Nightmare Begins Responsibility

Books by
MICHAEL S. HARPER

Nightmare Begins Responsibility
Debridement (1973)
Song: I Want a Witness (1972)
History as Apple Tree (1972)
History Is Your Own Heartbeat (1971)
Dear John, Dear Coltrane (1970)

NIGHTMARE
BEGINS RESPONSIBILITY

Michael S. Harper

UNIVERSITY OF ILLINOIS PRESS
Urbana   Chicago   London

Library of Congress Cataloging in Publication Data

Harper, Michael S.
  Nightmare begins responsibility.

  Poems.
  I.   Title.
PS3558.A6248N5   811'.5'4   74-10974
ISBN 0-252-00466-3
ISBN 0-252-00226-1 (pbk.)

Grateful acknowledgment is made to the following publications in which certain poems in this book first appeared: *Black World, Field, New Letters, World Order, Ohio Review, The New Yorker, Hoo Doo 3, Berkshire Review, A Singer in the Dawn* (Dodd, Mead), *Kansas City Star-Times.*

For: Shirl

'say it for two sons gone,
say nightmare, say it loud
panebreaking heartmadness:
nightmare begins responsibility.'

Contents

KIN

Kin 3
The Man Who Made Beds 5
Landfill 7
Tortilla Prayers 9
Leap 11
Seed 12
Move 14
China Ghost 16
Abe 17
Tucson 19
Witchcraft 20
From a Town in Minnesota 22
Called 24
Kin 2 26

APPROXIMATIONS

Playland: San Francisco 31
Someone to Claim: 'Don't Blame Me' 32
Memorial (Commencement) 33
Anthology: Black/White 34
Airborne 35
Poetry Concert 36
Holiday Inn 37
Primal Therapy 38
Iowa City: Letters 39
Buzzard's Roost: Briggs Stadium 41

CRYPTOGRAMS

Form 45
White Paper 46

Outer Visions 47
Amnesia 48
Amnesia 2 49
Essential Cryptogram 50
Care(s) 51
The Book of Names 52
Kingship 53
Dream as Reality 54
Daydream 55
1829/1830 56
Heartflow 57
The Essential Tree 58
Black Cryptogram 59
Surrender: Toomer(s) 60
Geese: The Passing of Harriet Tubman
    in the Night of First Ages 61

NIGHTMARE BEGINS RESPONSIBILITY

Grandfather 65
Blackjack 67
Buck 70
Alice Braxton Johnson 73
Roland 75
Nightmare Begins Responsibility 76

STERLING LETTERS

Br'er Sterling and the Rocker 79
Paul Laurence Dunbar: 1872–1906 80
Gains 81
mahalia: MAHALIA 83
Under the Posted Tree: Washington, DC 84
Wars: Debts: 'And When I Worries, I Sleeps' 85
BROWN at Brown 87

WILLIAMS COLLEGE: after 51 years — *89*
The Flowering of Garden: Self in Surrender *90*
Message to Robert Hayden *91*
No. 24 *92*
Corrected Review:
  THEREISATREEMOREANCIENTTHANEDEN *94*
Alice *96*

Kin

These are my first values: Understanding, Conscience, and Ability.
The moral functions are efforts toward the realization of true ideas and true aims.
Conscience, the heart of the human world, still beats feebly in our sense of decency.

Transformation is the spice of life transformed.

Man must add to nature. Effort is that which is added.
The aim of effort is to make it.

Let the doing be the exercise, not the exhibition.
Meet life's terms but never accept them.

'Straight, No Chaser' said the musician.

Kin

When news came that your mother'd
smashed her hip, both feet caught
in rungs of the banquet table,
our wedding rebroken on the memory
of the long lake of silence
when the stones of her body
broke as an Irish fence of stones,
I saw your wet dugs drag
with the weight of our daughter
in the quick of her sleep
to another feeding;
then the shoulders dropped
their broken antenna branches
of fear at the knife
running the scars
which had born into the colon
for the misspent enema,
the clubbed liver unclean
with the stones of the gall bladder,
and the broken arch of hip
lugging you to the lake,
the dough inner tube of lading
swollen with innerpatching.

I pick you up from the floor
of your ringing fears, the floor
where the photographs you have worked
into the cool sky of the gray you love,
and you are back at the compost pile
where the vegetables burn,
or swim in the storm of your childhood,
when your father egged you on with his
open machinery, the exhaust choking your sisters,
and your sisters choked still.

3

Now his voice stops you in accusation,
and the years pile up on themselves
in the eggs of your stretched sons,
one born on his birthday, both dead.
I pull you off into the sanctuary
of conciliation, of quiet tactics,
the uttered question, the referral,
which will quiet the condition you have seen
in your mother's shadow, the crutches
inching in the uncut grass,
and the worn body you will carry
as your own birthmark of his scream.

for Shirl

The Man Who Made Beds

He says his brother's son
died because the air force
called him to station
in a tornado
and a limb from a broken
tree cracked his neck;
when his wife
touched his shoulder
he was cold.

About his own children
he does not talk;
they run into flues
blackening their skins
as they whiten his hair
blackfaced in entertainment,
hooked on family
in Minnesota summer stream.

Freezing now
on locked lake-ice
the smoke rises
from fishhouses;
the black oaks
shimmer in ice
and break off:
bunks can be filled
with putty
as the man who makes beds
talks with his children
unanswered, fingers hammered,
arthritic bolts locked
in his sanded joints
where clear sticky varnish hides.

There is no more black oak
for fine furnishings;
the imperfect boards
cry on the jaws of horses;
a man talks to himself
where my children sleep,
unanswered and heard.

for Reuben Schultz

Landfill

Loads of trash and we light the match;
what can be in a cardboard box
can be in the bed of the pickup
and you jostle the containers onto the side road.
A match for this little road,
and a match for your son riding next to you firing,
and a match for the hole in the land filled with trees.
I will not mention concrete because theirs is the meshed
wire of concrete near the docks, and the concrete
of burned trees cut in cords of change-sawing,
and we will light a match to this too.

Work in anger for the final hour of adjustment
to the surveyors, and to the lawyers speaking of squatting,
and the land burning to no one.
This building of scrap metal, high as the storm that will break
it totally in the tornado dust,
and to the animals that have lived in the wheathay of their
    bedding
will beg for the cutting edge, or the ax,
or the electrified fencing that warms them in summer rain.

My son coughs on the tarred scrubble of cut trees,
and is cursed by the firelight, and beckoned to me to the pickup,
and washed of the soot of his sootskinned face,
and the dirt at the corners of my daughter's mouth will be
    trenchmouth;
and the worn moccasin of my woman will tear into the bulbed
    big toe,
and the blood will be black as the compost pile burning,
and the milk from her dugs will be the balm for the
    trenchmouth,
as she wipes her mouth from the smoke of the landfill filled
    with fire,

and these loads of trash will be the ashes for her to take:
and will be taken to the landfill, and filled, and filled.

for Shirl

Tortilla Prayers

Poet-drummer
in one skin,
brush strokes
of his grandmother
making tortillas
written on this brown face,
and his hands move
over pages of prayers
as he speaks of his daughters.

When he snares his life
in the poem for his grandmother,
his voice fades in the black
of his hand
poised on the blackboard sill,
the trapdrummed knuckles
cracking in this schoolroom
of maps and charts;

he says he was ashamed of her,
bandage-stockings,
scuffed marks where she shuffled
for his breakfast
as his thumbs shuttle
over a page of poems,
her childhood smallpox
killing her sisters,
the poem drumming its fingers
in her oily face,
skinned brown flour
while the hot grease pocks his skin brown.

In the car he says he will write
of his daughters,
twins from a single embrace,

his youngest by marriage;
and when he writes of them
she will unroll
her blanched stockings
and unplait her hair
where her flour smiles.

for Leonard Adame

Leap

Americo of the hunched face
of the Bronx
dancing on rooftops,
an unshaven face;
his laugh the laugh
of his mother
plucking silk of the garment
center, his breath
the fourth overdose
of dust whitened to flower
on the dress she wears
and ·will wear to her funeral
where he leaps
in the valley of her birth
in Puerto Rico
in the womb of the factory
where he was made
poet of our rooftops:
I call him brother
in his name, and in the dust he sniffs,
rooftops we will cross
with our fired lungs.

for Americo Casiano

Seed

When you said the universe
was a seed,
silence,
nothing at all,
that spirit-man
conjured it up
to make due with his life,
I only nodded,
and you said you were finished.
How many drinks
you'd had I didn't know
but I was told you'd been
that way, red-eyed, red-skinned
for three days,
and that your wife,
pregnant in Albuquerque,
had called you home.

How you knew to go
must have been that seed
you mentioned;
I hear your taped voice
parade up the pueblo
where you were born,
narratives of storms,
silently blossoming
as the child I imagine
will be born as you go home.

When I hear
you're not there
I think of the nothing at all
of the universe
that has sucked you

to its bosom of seed,
tight as the womb
your woman holds
after the birth of your son
in her small hands,
and think of the silence
of your voice,
lost in the airport
where the great birds
wriggle over the sierra
where you were born.

And still you are not home.
It is not drink that keeps
you away from she who calls,
nor your named sake;
it is a poem
written at the will-call,
the unbroken arrow
never broken,
and your son or daughter
clean as silence,
and your seed, yours.

Move

As he speaks
they drift off
and he says
'el barrio is different
in El Paso.'

3am breakfast
of eggs and bacon,
our toast the trucks
cruising downhill,
our waitress in black
on best behavior,
our third world shirts
stuck to our backs;
it must rain.

It does:
he tells me
again how it feels
to eat candy
after two shifts
in the cotton fields
and come out on parole
on insulin;

how he hungers
lost brothers
in the movement,
each shot
buried alive
hanged in his cell
eight hours before pardon
making him laugh;

as he laughs

he speaks of the campus
he lectured at,
his selling his brothers
three years hence,
how California
chicanos are different
from Texas.

Because he thinks that way
he writes in chicano
and gringo,
his pure Indian grandmother
his spoken family
in centuries of stone;

he speaks this language
to me, insulin breath
on his wife and children
west of El Paso;
and I speak back
in the black lake
breaking ground
in dry troughs
between Texas
and San Joaquin.

China Ghost

I first saw you running
after that poem of your mother
leaving, your father chasing
over the plains of China;

now you tell me she can't go home.
You tuck your sheaf of poems
into open strands of your face
housesitting for the summer.

Remember silkworm calm
vocals of your family,
pipe, silk clothes,
thin veins of jasmine in your ear:

hear all this in your chant
of that mountain that bore you open,
and is closing its windpipe,
and is calling your mother home.

for Mei Berssenbrugge

Abe

— *'I lost my last name at Ellis Island'* —

When you came back after your heart
stalled on the Chinese steps,
what street name in Prague,
does not matter;
what matters is your song
of great strain in our 30's
called hard times,
when great men of art
were workers from breads
their mothers made to sell,
and when they ate
they laughed, and what cheese
they got they paid for twice
in the same day
to the same man;
what roads their fathers
walked for work
we'll never know.

What we know is the price
one pays for indifference,
the shoed nail bent
into each soul to kick
at the arched movement,
each yarmulke poised to crow
on your wife whose name
comes clear as the belled charge
of Coltrane we will listen
to in the room of your daughter,
her son the book
written as your heart
pours liquid fumes

of the life he must know,
and what the bread cost,
what you paid
to keep the stairwell
unchambered, unbypassed,
a red road open
at the crossroad
of scarred hands.

for Abe and Belle Chapman

Tucson

The podium beveled,
its sound the poem
where my sons stand
in this aisle; Mary sobs:
christian
at their tombs,
rose-face open and flowing —
or pagan, her mesa-face
shut at Phoenix airport
departing in bare feet —
or my woman stocking
compost to cure her loss
in great berries flowering
in the rain.

With silver bird
brought for her that bore
these sons, hung
in creases of her smock,
cactus pricking her belly,
sons I see calling
in my night of torn gems:
in this furrow shaken
I take hold.

for Shirl

Witchcraft

'A witch is a woman of no heart;
A heart broken is a witch.'

You change your name
making identity,
and I hear you've stolen
your daughter's heart,
her eight-year-old body
empty with your image
crying for mother;
six others catheter
their open wounds
insulting who's born
them in your masquerade,
for I'm told you were never
honest, that you looked
for father in priest,
professor, the man you married.

I see you in costume:
face lined with ink
etchings of greased
hair breaking in kerchief.

The demon steals mystery
at birth, confession,
communion, barnyard prowls
toward puberty
where your eggs
riverbottom,
day and night,
Mississippi-Illinois
in telephone therapy.

What I tell you,

20

listening, is the poem
I will not write
for the open page of heart
stolen: it is simply
interfacing:
human happenstance;
human kindness:

You are a witch debunked
tasting seven missing parts.

From a Town in Minnesota

"GUN: 'from the feminine in which both names mean WAR'"

One side tight in the case,
scope screwed on my head,
brown stock like my owner
unfiring, prepared;
bought from deadly shot
who went berserk in Newport,
I crept into Oakland
in a back seat
of a friend
who later gave up games
with dumdum shell
in his temple
but I was sleeping
on this top shelf
cuddled from explosion.

You want to borrow
me for a hunt
in Kenai,
and uncased
I loosen my handle
sight off center
tightening my strap
on your blade of flesh
I will hold on long
treks through berries
where the moose lie.

I go back to sleep
carried over frontiers
of clothing I lie among,
my master's grandfather
naked on the firing

22

range, his blue hat
broken at brim;
and know I will
awaken decades from here,
waiting for answers
that never speak to me,
cartridges
of an enemy
part stranger,
greased, armpit anchored,
waiting for the burned flit
of hair trigger
pulled toward the closet,
these skeletons I wear.

Digging the grave
through black dirt,
gravel and rocks
that will hold her down,
we speak of her heat
which has driven her out
over the highway
in her first year.

A fly glides from her mouth
as we take her four legs,
and the great white neck
mudded at the lakeside
bends gracefully into the arc
of her tongue, colorless, now,
and we set her in the bed
of earth and rock
which will hold her as the sun
sets over her shoulders.

You had spoken of her brother,
100 lbs or more,
and her slight frame
from the diet of chain
she had broken;
on her back
as the spade cools her brow
with black dirt, rocks,
sand, white tongue,
what pups does she hold
that are seeds unspayed
in her broken body;
what does her brother say
to the seed gone out over

the prairie, on the hunt
of the unreturned:
and what do we say
to the master of the dog dead,
heat, highway, this bed
on the shoulder
of the road west
where her brother called, calls.

Kin 2

— *one more time* — *(unblue version)*

When news came that your mother'd
smashed her hip, both feet caught
in rungs of the banquet table,
our wedding rebroken on the memory
of the long lake of silence
when the stones of her body
broke as an Irish fence of stones,
I see your wet dugs drag
with the weight of our daughter
in the quick of her sleep
to another feeding.

I pick you up from the floor
of your ringing fears, the floor
where the photographs you have worked
cool into the sky of the gray you love,
and you are back at the compost pile
where the vegetables burn,
or swim in the storm of your childhood,
when your father egged you on with his
open machinery, the exhaust choking your sisters,
and your sisters choked still.

Now the years pile up on themselves,
and his voice stops you in accusation,
in the eggs of your stretched sons,
one born on his birthday, both dead.
I pull you off into the sanctuary
of conciliation, of quiet tactics,
the uttered question, the referral,
which will quiet the condition you have seen
in your mother's shadow, the crutches

inching in the uncut grass,
and the worn body you will carry
as your own birthmark of his scream.

for Shirl

Approximations:

for RALPH A(LBERT) DICKEY, 1946–1972

'the plastic bag is only the final envelope' —

— your hair's so nappy
  who's your pappy
  you're some ugly child —

'once upon a time in the Land of Mush
lived a carpenter named Crush;
he made boxes, little boxes,
square boxes and round boxes,
smooth boxes and lumpy boxes,
but most of all empty boxes'
                    — RAD —

'arcanum blues: the mystery of the unspoken word
spoken on the breath of the unanswerable answer
answered in the name of the unnamed namesaken
self(lessness), moonstruck, signifying transcendent
manifestation of essential oneness whole in the
absence of self in the unity of nothingness
everywhere, night/death/devil/angel tension of
opposites black/white essential you/me/we.'

Playland: San Francisco

Come back to us
in your good looks,
so young, the hairs on your face
glow;
I have a bulletin
from the coroner
what I have is your journal
of boxes,
the music of your spheres
in my trained head:
Listen, you can hear me
'Round Midnight' singing
"it is midnight here," *mf*
and we are talking
in the poem you wrote to us
in Syracuse
and all references to piano
keys, white and black.

Someone to Claim: 'Don't Blame Me'

It is important to teach
by example,
as you did,
your face smooth,
your hair so curled
in antennae
no one would believe, even you,
interfaced without proof —
give us
poison for snails,
plastic bags over head,
all your belongings:
at midnight
immanence and transcendence
merge in the essential
parked car
near the ocean
light and darkness
the spray
and the lesson taught.

Memorial (Commencement)

We must conjure you
with poems; you come from Berkeley
hills moving little,
conifers, eucalyptus,
a daughter named Chanta
not your daughter
where your daughter lives.

white   Wanted to be poet
so, yes you did;
and it came to you in night
frost of summer,
skies full of mist,
women crying in studios,
lost wigs,
mirrors gone:

black   dreamed of poetry
you'd never written,
needed writing,
began, all at once,
to do the job in ten days,
or dying, see the dream
real in the roasted body
of work
strewn on the body of woman,
a woman of no name.

black   Now your woman has left you,
three weeks gone, quiet
smoke breaking over
worn ribbons won't let you cry;

white   when it is cold
it will be cold in studio,
hair false
hair though it grows,
mirror its own
table for writing;

and you will write her moistened
back into its burnt side.

Airborne

And there is the box,
it flies in the belly
jet plane for Detroit:
for the city you died in
and for your mother unseen
and for your friends unspoken
and this box is empty with your body.

We remember you
calling America
on the phone:
frontal friends from college
who worked in animal ecstasy,
hypos in the animal hotel;
the drenched finger of syrup
you took up in a high,
that high gone
in the papers of the factory
in its oily cones,
'Detroit, please'
and our fingers dialing:
you called it primal,
the code your scream,
and on the assembly line
of Cadillac I heard you sigh.

Holiday Inn

We call your silent
mother,
buried in the watchful belt
undoing her poisoned waters:
we must blame whatever it speaks
to her image,
whitened in a Finnish calm;
to your dark father
gone home in uniform,
your grey eyes sparkling
in the candles of your mother's apron,
is your dark father's hair,
and it curls necklength
on the windpipe where you
can't go home.
This spigot where you hang
drips on her sugared apron:
now you can go home,
and your father is the carpenter
who left you not in the box
that carried your body home
to Detroit,
and your mother is not
at the door of this Inn:

and as you scream
it is not primal
and the race
split down the twin
circling roads
on whitened family
have no beds,
and this is a hotel
where you told me this inn-counter.

Primal Therapy

You are your first scream;
we know that from whites
at the table of your body;
the wine is black wine
as they toast you.

I am your last breath,
my name scribbled on the postcard
near your shriveled head,
and in the cake you crave,
your hand on my hand
writing the job you couldn't do
on your own body:
to split the child of the first scream
with the child of the last breath:

you are your last breath;
you are your first scream:
you are; you are.

Iowa City: Letters

While reading African
novels you wrote
you loved them most
for the twin souls,
one real, one dwelling
in the spirit world;
that you were without
one, being neither white
nor black, and therefore
whole in the knowledge
there was no place
where you could lie;
the space of woman,
neither loose nor tight,
comforted this half part
walking the night
you lived in
perched over pin-ball,
a quarter jukebox
where a woman
always white
would shoot the last
ball, and now drunk
you failed loving her
completely,
and went to your own home
tired, unfinished,
your other half singing
on your shoulder
where her hand rested
and where your poems,
half-finished, failed.

Fence-sitting on racial
stakes of culture:
woman as poem,
you at the piano playing,
the hermetic mode
sealing you in.

Buzzard's Roost: Briggs Stadium

You won this contest
playing Beethoven
while your family
cheered:
'They told me not
to take anything
from his Volvo;
I slipped out
letters, poems, journals,
notebooks crammed in belongings,
his living primal manual;
he's ours to bury
though in summer his face
complex and funky
was strong as sunlight,
the stiff twirls of hair
standing tall;
in November,
that primal shuck,
three weeks, journal
agonies, the-rapist
sucking his instincts
untrusting his body's house.'

'Blowing' in a baseball stadium;
writing the arcane poem
when his mother let him go,
when his father never came.

"The primary cause of disorder
in ourselves
is the seeking of reality
promised by another";

'is it not possible to explode
from one's center'
you asked of no one:
John Doe, alias Ralph A(lbert)
Dickey, we're watching centerfield:
you've won your contest
in this last, primal scream.

Cryptograms

For ROBERT C. TOWNS
and in memory of *jean toomer* (EUGENE PINCHBACK TOOMER)

Man is a being potentially able to act with reason according to value.

We should have both actuality and potentiality: a sense of reality.

Caring alone produces events of force.

Men are most active when evading real issues,
* most powerful when rejecting real values.*

Man is a nerve of the cosmos, dislocated, trying to quiver into place.

A true individual belongs, on the one hand, to no less than himself;
* and, on the other, to no less than mankind and the entire*
* human world.*

I am of the field of being.

We do not possess imagination enough to sense what we are missing.

Human relationships are matters of skill and art.

We who have almost enough knowledge to separate the atom may fail
* to separate men from their antagonisms.*

The human world wants to hear what is wrong with it.

Man is a prejudice to himself.

Aim to use insanity as a means of developing reason.

By exhausting your ordinary surface force you will be compelled to
* learn to use your magical deep force.*

A conflict wastes energy; a tension generates it.

We move and hustle but lack rhythm.

Morality is the determination not to be determined.

We should have a living spirit and the ability to spiritualize experience.

Perceptions of reality are man's main food.

There are only two things in the universe: significance, and the possibility
* of understanding it.*

The need is to find a method for developing essence and perfecting being.

(from ESSENTIALS by Jean Toomer)

Form

the decadent
reduction
to the inhuman
in
non-functional
terms.

White Paper

The dream to forgiveness
is the back broken
on the bridge
of too short a body.

Outer Visions

Heaven is below one's waist;
hell above one's neck.

Split infinitives
reduced to form(s).

Amnesia

To forget God
in yourself
is to forget self
and defame God
yourself.

Man is what he thought
he believed,
didn't do,
and what he became
his undoing.

Beauty not of itself
is unseen,
of self unspoken,
unheard denied
never lost.

Care(s)

'Man is created for the purpose of active participation in Divine Intellect, of which he is the central reflection.'

When earth is crater
the heavens cysted smoke
water a fibrous tank
the heart itself bypass:
bypass mined.

The Book of Names

By habit
cultivate your name;
the dead spoken
remembered habitual.

Kingship

Pray: when the soul's
on its knees;
dream: as body runs
upright;
work: when worlds
turn manward;
love: when the image
is not your own.

The secret self
is the most public man
speaking;
the most open man
the public self unheard:
the private voice open publicity,
silence the heard music.

Daydream

Success measured through obstacles
is the road to success;
man's place his choice
to do great things,
be his belief,
in factual dreams,
dreamed.

1829/1830

— *'Andrew Jackson's answer to petitions*/THE TRAIL OF TEARS'—

Injury soothed by woman;
her rainbow trail
bowed seed of children
spawned in invisible sound,
beyond music,
the soul its heartbeat,
beating;
when sorrow knocks
the door stands open,
is taken in,
visible,
boomeranged at hearth,
pestle,
the spooned crooning of no fear,
new face,
the child of earth
on the hurtful occasion.

Heartflow

The present of yourself
is the friend you need most;
the present of another loved
is masterpiece of selflessness:
befriend, the heart flows open;
deny, the tomb is closed.

The Essential Tree

Greatness in life is spending
it for something that will outlast life,
and be life renewed in other lives:
the death of death
is illusory;
the death of life
an enigma.

Black Cryptogram

When God
created
the black child
He was
showing off.

for Sterling A. Brown

Surrender: Toomer(s)

'The theme of Cosmic Violation in Toomer's CANE.*'*

Earth
Art
Music
unchained/
mulatto
remains

Geese: The Passing of Harriet Tubman
in the Night of First Ages

— 'In the beginning was the word and the denial of the word' —

*'The mystery of geese: a goose blindfolded hits the target,
given inner concentration and inward union with timeless
essence, as physical transmutations are signs outward,
though inwardly holy, once inner work is completed.'*

By habit cultivate your names;
the deeds spoken remembered habitual:
flocks, Harriet's.

Nightmare Begins Responsibility

An artist is he who can balance strong contrasts, who can combine opposing forms and forces in significant unity.

'what polishes the heart is the invocation of God, and in his name'

for my parents: Katherine Johnson Harper
Walter Warren Harper

Grandfather

In 1915 my grandfather's
neighbors surrounded his house
near the dayline he ran
on the Hudson
in Catskill, NY
and thought they'd burn
his family out
in a movie they'd just seen
and be rid of his kind:
the death of a lone black
family is *the Birth*
of a Nation,
or so they thought.
His 5'4" waiter gait
quenched the white jacket smile
he'd brought back from watered
polish of my father
on the turning seats,
and he asked his neighbors
up on his thatched porch
for the first blossom of fire
that would burn him down.

They went away, his nation,
spittooning their torched necks
in the shadows of the riverboat
they'd seen, posse decomposing;
and I see him on Sutter
with white bag from your
restaurant, challenged by his first
grandson to a foot-race
he will win in white clothes.

I see him as he buys galoshes

for his railed yard near Mineo's
metal shop, where roses jump
as the el circles his house
toward Brooklyn, where his rain fell;
and I see cigar smoke in his eyes,
chocolate Madison Square Garden chews
he breaks on his set teeth,
stitched up after cancer,
the great white nation immovable
as his weight wilts
and he is on a porch
that won't hold my arms,
or the legs of the race run
forwards, or the film
played backwards on his grandson's eyes.

Blackjack

1963;
we march.

I look out remedial
white windowed essays
from Pasadena
I will read tonight
and there you are visiting
three black sisters
excluded from official parade
'their skins unlovely.'

Orange and Fair Oaks
to grow on
to the stadium
blocks where you stand
silent; I am silent —

Nodding I say
'47 high noon in the bleachers,
Cards in town,
you jog the outfield grass
lagging loose balls,
how you lofted their cream-
skinned signatures
over the white heads
where we sat pigeontoed
circling their dugout,
how we carried your curled
name to our table
while your team cursed
your singed garters
on pennant flagged tongues.

As they saw nothing

but your teeth and eyes
we saw the jeering train
unwinding its sheets in Georgia,
your mail cringing with snake
juice spat in the Bronx;
and when you crossed
our borders we cheered
our black ace
of the marked deck of Westwood,
the bowl we stand in,
the counter where their salted
nuts stack in their vacuum cans.

We will not speak of broad
jumps over tracks,
yardlines of pigskin
jaunted, stitched white balls
spiked at your skull:
we will remember the found
sleep and meals you lost
running over bases
their pitchers feared covering,
balls you made them eat
now flowering from your son's
funeral car.

High blood pressure,
diabetes,
your eyes gone blind,
I will not answer.
I steel home
at your back
down the red clay road
of their stadium
recalling Rachel,

my own daughter,
on deck.

"Did he say Blackie?"
my brother said
of the white boy
in row G:
'Black Jack,
the gamble's taken,
the debt unpaid,
and the answer,
answered, still to come.'

for Jackie Robinson

Buck

I owe him for pictures
of champions I'd known,
or never seen,
or never known
and seen as men like
him, arched now
on a drunk
to ease arthritis,
his red tie
soaked in vomit,
his blue-ringed eyes
etched in glaucoma,
menace in serge-body
on his day off
near the cubicle
where he polishes
shoes, downtown
handballers at this Y.

Tomorrow
he will kneel
over the soft leather
of his polished nails,
his glasses pouched
as two black circles,
past years at sea,
his prison blindness,
concessions lost
to three promoters
the night Joe Louis
broke in the garden;
that he could box Sugar
in his prime,
hit like Archie,

teach Gavilan to bolo,
all this in signed
photos of his gallery,
is his hangover and cure
of the future of brushes.

Four bits,
he's changed men into boys
when they ask of his photos,
black and greased
in red velvet,
buckdancing in high-topped shoes,
he'll tell a lawyer
his two cushions
are his hero chamber;
'even with glasses off
I can tell you're a boy.'
He'll speak of his father
in Panama, lost and broken
in the canal
where ships cruise
to Frisco
keelhauling his shadow,
how he followed
his known sister
who'd died ironing
his suit cleaned
on her kitchen benches.

When my third son
died in intensive,
after early birth,
he took two photos
of his champions
for two sons I'd lost,

and signed their backs;
patting my shoulder
with mahogany nails
he called them grandsons,
turned toward two men
with black, unlaced shoes
patting their sleeping soles.

Alice Braxton Johnson

We lift your weight from chair
to bed to bedpan to chair to windowsill
as you stroke your way
from third floor infirmary windows
of our home;
I walk tearless to school
forgetting your name.

When you sit up all night
in your chair waiting for your children
to come, holding their ginwheel caravan
of parties, roughnecks following to beat
your son: trumpet-playing playboy Barrett
would call to the window in hazy
first light: "you there, Mom?";
and you always were.

So my mother nursed you over
years heart-stroked to the coalcar
of cemetery unnamed in my memory
but for the large kitchen where you reigned
hovering children, grandchildren plucked.
Your son, Barrett, would hold me loosening
in the '46 Ford from Rome to Brooklyn
breaking the limit —
as he was to die leaving Rome
in the hazy morning ride
driven off the road
in a favor for a friend.

Did you save these roughnecks
who hated his laugh
when they rode him into the marked tree;
did you know he was to follow
you in his coalcar of our family?

I watch his black sole plant
his size twelve foot jamming
the gas, my eight-year-old hands
at his wheel, his fight with my mother
in mortgages, my mother's weight
on the seasoned floor of the moon,
the moon bleeding onto linoleum,
my father's face in the transom
where I was born, your house
torpedoed on my tearless walk to school,
and this chair empty.

Roland

— *a tune of watchfulness* —

They told me to sit on the highest stool,
eating ice cream to my grandfather's
beckoning, his hands batons of light,
knuckles chiseled in saving
his people without money.

Who waits for the watch that a white man
brought to our stoop some weeks after
his stitches healed, his eye put back
from the sidewalk glimmering with vision,
his wrecked car cleaned from the corner
where he stacked his flesh
put back by a black man from Canada?

'moments of your life
added years to mine'
the watch says to my son
named for the man who wove
the eye back in its socket,
who drew me from my mother
in the upstairs infirmary bedroom,
who pointed to my mole
marked for his father.

To the white man
interfaced on the streetcorner:
a toast from the highest stool
from whenever my son sits wheeling
in his own chair ticking;
and to Roland, to Roland,
this word from his seat
of ancestral force
on his feeding frequency
of the high mode.

Nightmare Begins Responsibility

I place these numbed wrists to the pane
watching white uniforms whisk over
him in the tube-kept
prison
fear what they will do in experiment
watch my gloved stickshifting gasolined hands
breathe *boxcar-information-please* infirmary tubes
distrusting white-pink mending paperthin
silkened end hairs, distrusting tubes
shrunk in his *trunk-skincapped*
shaven head, in thighs
distrusting-white-hands-picking-baboon-light
on this son who will not make his second night
of this wardstrewn intensive airpocket
where his father's asthmatic
hymns of *night-train*, train done gone
his mother can only know that he has flown
up into essential calm unseen corridor
going boxscarred home, *mamaborn, sweetsonchild
gonedowntown* into *researchtestingwarehousebatteryacid
mama-son-done-gone*/me telling her 'nother
train tonight, no music, no breathstroked
heartbeat in my infinite distrust of them:

and of my distrusting self
white-doctor-who-breathed-for-him-all-night
say it for two sons gone,
say nightmare, say it loud
panebreaking heartmadness:
nightmare begins responsibility.

Sterling Letters:

for STERLING A. BROWN

When God created the black child, he was showing off —
'He may mean good but he do so doggone po' —
'You run them verbs; I'll drive the thought' —

'Lemme be wid John Henry, steel drivin' man,
    Lemme be wid old Jazzbo,
       Lemme be wid ole Jazzbo. . . .

(from 'Odyssey of Big Boy'
by Sterling A. Brown)

  'The strong men keep a-comin' on
  The strong men git stronger.'

(from 'Strong Men'
by Sterling A. Brown)

'Great God, but he was a man'

'Den take yo' time. . . .
Honey, take yo' bressed time.'

(from 'Strong Men'
by Sterling A. Brown)

Br'er Sterling and the Rocker

Any fool knows a Br'er in a rocker
is a boomerang incarnate; look at the blade
of the rocker, that wondrous crescent
rockin' in harness as poem.

To speak of poetry is the curled line straightened;
to speak of doubletalk, the tongue
gone pure, the stoic line a trestle
whistlin', a man a train comin' on:

Listen Br'er Sterling
steel-drivin' man, folk-said, folk-sayin',
that chair's a blues-harnessed star
turnin' on its earthy axis;

Miss Daisy, latch on that star's arc,
hold on sweet mama; Br'er Sterling's rocker glows.

for Sterling A. and Daisy T. Brown
16 June 1973

Paul Laurence Dunbar: 1872–1906

One hundred years of headrags, bandages,
plantation tradition gone sour;
in the smokehouse, Newport, RI
a knotted metaphor collapsed in foyer,
Miss Ann finally understanding the elevator
where you sang your standard
imperfect lyrics.

Minstrel and mask:
a landscape of speech and body
burned in verbal space,
the match cinder unstandard:
double-conscious brother in the veil —
double-conscious brother in the veil:
double-conscious brother in the veil.

— *written on the 100th anniversary of his*
   birth, in continuum, in modality — Dayton, Ohio: 1972

Gains

His voice soothes;
though his letters
are illegible
and unmailed
one gets the flow
from the trees
he describes,
or the uncle
who drank;
and when he died,
the uncle finer
than others of his
family, we must
believe the writer,
so I believe.

I see him on his gallery,
chinaball loping
in twilight, the old
folks telling
the dust as it settles
the night will be
cool, the humming insects
caressing bushes
blossoming like stars
named for women
on the slackened porch
in the weight of shoes
that stand open
to the dusky air.

How they speak are lines
in his books,
washed in the river never crossed,

or the tree whose shadow
roots underground,
or the chair that holds
an aunt who never walked
but raised his family,
her sky the sister
who faded as a voice
from the swamp
that packed her man
east of the small town
near the plantation
where you were born.

You come back home
to see tight arrows
of torn orchards
fruit-stubborn and thorned,
and you come back twice
to the river where the old
uncle talked, to bottles
stocked in *your* room
where the arms of his chair
cradled your stories
as they filled the air:
what is lost is his voice
in your voice; gained in
what you say and do.

for Ernest J. Gaines

mahalia: MAHALIA

— *'a voice like hers comes along*
once a millennium' — *MLK, Jr.*

High-pitched waves of glory
bring you down in Chicago;
though satan should be bound
and it is spring
the death of him
inspired, dreamed
in glory to Memphis,
your choired practice
this spirit bowl-flesh
rouged echoing full faces
torn in shakes of saving —
her transcendent voice.

Words, sungstrewn, always the last word:
high-pitched resonant
whole sister fortified in Jesus
here in these deathmarch horsedrawn
blessings: most hearty bedrocked
sister with bad heart weakening
our ecstatic pain:

and who is listening?
head-dressed high-pitched whole sister
in the choir-chariot down
who is listening to your name.

Under the Posted Tree: Washington, DC

— Sister Goose was swimming on the lake —

Demented, dream-eyed
headragged woman,
pestle of keys,
doors unopened,
illiterate Harriet
asleep under her staked tree:
dead or alive
mumbling over John Brown's
vision under her sign
unreadable living posted tree.

Sister Rose Anne, Miss Daisy-Harriet
lighter than skinned trees
where your father's hats hang,
your grandma crying for geese
caught in the fox-weeded reeds,
so she took him to court:
Rose Anne talks through Harriet's
derangement tacked to her forehead,
illegitimate, illiterate
sweet-mama-wise.

Sister Goose got her trial
in the den-park, under her sign
after fair sentencing
her bones on these witness stands:
all foxes.
Daisy sings to her grandmother,
Sister Goose, swimming on the lake,
demanding justice, sweet geese,
these headragged readable sisters
asleep, their deranged wants
dead and alive.

Insomnia is your cocktail
tobacco, records, books
marked on loveseat, ironing board.

Didn't he ramble'
in highwire breezed Berkshires
gambling in innocence,
the gunnery the long road
you walk in your father's shoes.

Your children all legitimate
in their touching you when you stopped
writing poems for their classroom;
they rise, pipesmoke flues you stoked
filling with kindling.

Deep, thorough, the conspiracy
to silence you they will not know;
your allies drop from disease,
dying quietly in retirement
behind the lines. On these you stand.

Sons, daughters, honor you.
From nearest perch they wait word,
laughing in mourning at your tales.

Some things must be told to be remembered:
that you taught in kingship; Mrs. Bibbie,
'Big Boy' Davis, J. C. Moreland, Sporting Daniels;
that you rode the trains, conceived in church:
listen, it is late, frost polishes
these keys in the *cabaret*
where the mockingbirds lie;

we have built off you,
we have stolen from you,
we have loved you and must tell you so,
just in time
always too late.

BROWN at Brown

— *Brown University, April 1973* —

You peer over books
looking for citations:
Tom, Liza, Jim 'live
in your wired orbs
fired in pitted coalcars.

Broken guitar, restrung
and hung on the sidings where you limp
over cork from our fast freight
looking for the ungrammatical
in the unseen mine.

Where are you now
but in Georgia looking for a man
unstrung and old yet singing
of the unmilked snake
of ancestors, a bloody
crop soaked in turpentine.

Somewhere are images of women
called Virginia;
this winding train
mothers the wife
you hold, her fear
is your fear, yours
the truth she is,
and in her image you will write.

What books you have in your razored
doubletalk will not be written;
what you instruct will not be learned.
Though this mask glimmers of manhood
fading in the train you ride
(letters written will cloak

this truth, this passion
angered interface).

it is necessary that you break
to be tested in what you do,
and as you break there is your song,
and in straight tongue
is this doubletalk of our love:
you surrender, your suffering
made intentional in your word,
and on this day the word is given,
your word in our phenomenal bodies.

Of course you have fought
in language for what was real
about us, your mama's jim crow
fight on Howard's campus,
dozens in the half dozen
children she bore,
your father's facts
reborn in you, and you
fighting to be born in self,
transcending your poems
on traintracks bottomless
in Foggy Bottom,
pain and laughter of your people
in your people's word.
You sustain us,
comic tragedy, yarns,
our spayed ancestors,
and you their singer.

We love you in your unwillingness
to apologize for us,
for our passing in the great civil
war where we understood ourselves,
creating ourselves in what our fathers
thought, hoped; pickax, gang, field:
tongues ungrammatical and wise.

You wouldn't let us lose our form,
its energy of purpose, the speech of meaning
in deeds broken in the written word.
And you are broken and remade
here in Williamstown,
the great wreck of spirit
torn into images of what you made
in language, the word always ours.

The Flowering of Garden:
Self in Surrender

You lie down in damp flower bed
stiff hip dancing to blossom
scented hands to judgment:
no birth cradled without pain
no apology for essential contact,
your earth-tongued ancestored
grandmother
arthritic with wet loam.

Was slavery surrender tending
these scented thorned hips,
their bloodbed broken fruit
illegal and refined
in your smile-breaking hinges
and you open in essential bloom?

for Rose Anne 'Daisy' T. Brown
21 January 1974

Message to Robert Hayden

Do I make connections
only after Arna's death
electric with thanks
for his warning loud
handclasp on the porch
weight, waiting in Nashville
words of power lines
down, sparks invisible;

lying, locked in your car,
Erma's keyed night visit.
And now, thanks,
the only death that makes
this message riddling
praise of musing
over wires, down, always down:
and we bury that spark to light, always to light.

As you read your comics
she circles her left wrist,
thumb and forefinger,
nodding to friends;
your high voice caroms
in your coke bottle,
her alcohol stripping adhesive
from your gimpy knee;
though her fingers strike
matches on your fibrous biceps
it is waist, hips, thighs
she wears on frothy lips.

What of the centerfield wall?
She shrinks flammable
on your streaked uniform
where blood dries
on hipless pants.

Do not forget Birmingham:
we did not cry
but saw you shorten your open
stance for the hop
of eaten stitches:
Candlestick and Shea
your forelegs
broken in confetti.

Do not unhook your tongue-
broken grammar with commercials;
do not sell your restricted
billboard home secure.

Cup your hands
in familiar basket,

put your white suit
in her mitt
for she is there.
Her tubes stroke your evening
for the bat you wield:

she smiles with presents,
her wrists, fingers,
remembering what you were.
We fill your name in our space,
cokes and comics
on our shadowed wall.

for Willie Mays

Corrected Review:
THEREISATREEMOREANCIENTTHANEDEN

> 'The tree is unique, qualitatively speaking, and cannot be subject
> to purely quantitative comparison; it is impossible to reduce the
> world of sense-perceptions to quantitative categories. Qualitative
> things do not belong to matter, which is merely mirror for it,
> so it can be seen, but not so that it can be altogether limited
> to the material plane.'

> 'Man is created for the purpose of active participation in Divine
> Intellect, of which he is the central reflection.'

From the *source* comes the imagery and language,
compassion and complexity in the *one*
achieved in the imagination conjured,
admired in surrender and transcendence:
where is the *perfect* man?

Words beyond words to conjure this malaise
to infamy and death in effort
immanence forsaken:
to blow the music
maelstrom-tempered.

Our mode is our jam session
of tradition,
past in this present moment
articulated, blown through
with endurance,
an unreaching extended
improvised love of past masters,
instruments technically down:

structured renderings of reality
our final war with self;
rhetoric/parlance arena-word-consciousness:
morality: man to man

man to god
in a tree
more ancient than eden.

for Leon Forrest

Alice

'The word made stone, the stone word'
'A RITE *is an action the very form of which is the result of a Divine Revelation.'*

I

You stand waist-high in snakes
beating the weeds for the gravebed
a quarter mile from the nearest
relative, an open field in Florida: lost,
looking for Zora, and when she speaks
from her sunken chamber to call
you to her side, she calls
you her distant cousin, her sister
come to mark her burial place
with bright black stone.
She has known you would do this —
her crooked stick, her straight lick —
and the lie you would have to tell
to find her, and that you lied
to her relatives in a conjure-riddle
of the words you have uttered,
calling her to communion.

A black rock of ages you have placed
where there was no marker,
and though the snakes abound
in this preserve from ancestral space,
you have paid your homage
in traditional line, the face open:
your face in the woman-light of surrender
toughened in what you were.

II

Floods of truth flow from your limbs
of these pages in a vision swollen
in experience and pain:
that child you stepped into blossom
of a man's skull beaten into smile
of submission, you gathering horse nectar
for offering over a baby's crusted gasp,
for centuries of motherhood and atonement
for which you write, and the rite written.

And for this I say your name: Alice,
my grandmother's name, your name,
conjured in snake-infested field
where Zora Neale welcomed you home,
and where I speak from now
on higher ground of her risen
black marker where you have written
your name in hers, and in mine.

for Alice Walker

Poetry from Illinois

History Is Your Own Heartbeat
Michael S. Harper (1971)

The Foreclosure
Richard Emil Braun (1972)

The Scrawny Sonnets and Other Narratives
Robert Bagg (1973)

The Creation Frame
Phyllis Thompson (1973)

To All Appearances: Poems New and Selected
Josephine Miles (1974)

Nightmare Begins Responsibility
Michael S. Harper (1975)

The Black Hawk Songs
Michael Borich (1975)